The Life of a
TURTLE

Clare Hibbert

Chicago, Illinois

Printed and bound in China by the South China
Printing Company

08 07 06 05 04
10 9 8 7 6 5 4 3 2 1

Library of Congress Cataloging-in-Publication
Data

Hibbert, Clare, 1970-
    The life of a turtle / Clare Hibbert.
        p. cm. -- (Life cycles)
    Includes bibliographical references (p.   ) and
index.
    ISBN 1-4109-0546-2 (lib. bdg. : hardcover)
    1. Loggerhead turtle--Life cycles--Juvenile
literature. I. Title. II. Series: Hibbert, Clare, 1970-
Life cycles.
    QL666.C536H53 2004
    597.92--dc22

                        2004002719

Acknowledgments
The publishers would like to thank the following
for permission to reproduce photographs:p. 4
Minden Pictures/FLPA; p. 5 Portfield
Chickering/Science Photo Library; p. 8 Peter
Chadwick; p. 9 Daryl Balfour; p. 10 Jean Paul
Ferrero/Ardea; p. 11 John L. Pontier/Oxford
Scientific Films; p. 12 V. and W.
Brandon/Imagequest 3-D; p. 13 Anthony
Bannister/NHPA; pp. 14, 15 Natural Visions;
p. 16 Norbert Wu/NHPA; p. 17 Lynda
Richardson/Corbis; p. 18 Adrian Warren/Ardea;
p. 19, 25 Gerard Lacz/FLPA; p. 20 Norbert
Wu/Minden Pictures/FLPA; p. 21 Corbis; p. 22
Daniel Heuclin/NHPA; p. 23 Howard Hall/Oxforad
Scientific Films; p. 24 Ron and Valerie
Taylor/Ardea; p. 26 ANT Photolibrary; p. 27
Stan Osolinski; p. 28 Lynn Stone; p. 29 Adrian
Davies/Nature Picture Library.

Cover photograph of a loggerhead turtle,
reproduced with permission of FLPA
(Minden Pictures).

The publishers would like to thank Janet Stott for
her assistance in the preparation of this book.

Every effort has been made to contact copyright
holders of any material reproduced in this book.
Any omissions will be rectified in subsequent
printings if notice is given to the publishers.

Contents

Any words appearing in bold, **like this,** are explained in the Glossary.

Loggerhead Turtles

Turtles are **reptiles** that spend most of their lives in water. Like all reptiles, turtles have a bony **skeleton** and scaly skin. Turtle babies **hatch** from eggs that are laid on land. They look just like their parents, only much smaller.

This baby loggerhead turtle is hatching from its egg. It has flippers and a shell, just like an adult turtle.

Growing up

Just as you grow bigger year after year, a turtle grows and changes, too. The different stages of the turtle's life make up its **life cycle.** There are several different types of turtle, but they all have similar life cycles. This book is about the life cycle of a loggerhead turtle. Loggerheads have big, bony heads.

Where loggerheads live

The place where an animal lives is called its habitat. Loggerhead turtles are found in warm oceans and seas, where there are plenty of **shellfish,** crabs, and sea urchins to eat.

Loggerheads live in warm waters.

A Turtle's Life

The **life cycle** of a turtle begins when a female comes on shore to lay her eggs. When the eggs **hatch,** the baby turtles scramble down to the ocean. The next part of their life is a mystery, because they are rarely seen. Young loggerheads hide and feed among the seaweed that floats on ocean **currents.**

After six years or more, the turtles return to the coastline. There they grow even bigger, until they are old enough to **mate.** They travel thousands of miles back to their nesting grounds, where the females lay their eggs.

Loggerhead life span

Some loggerheads live to be 100 years old, but few live that long. Many are eaten by other animals or caught in fishing nets.

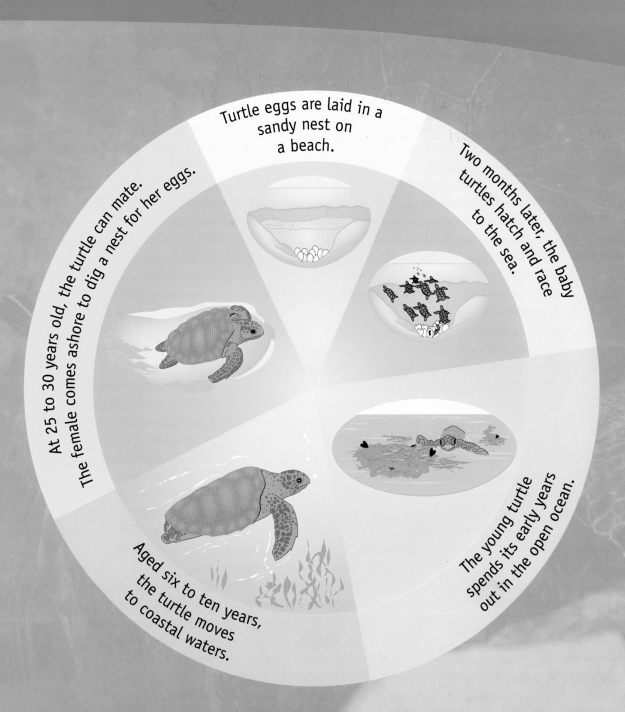

Turtle eggs are laid in a sandy nest on a beach.

Two months later, the baby turtles hatch and race to the sea.

The young turtle spends its early years out in the open ocean.

Aged six to ten years, the turtle moves to coastal waters.

At 25 to 30 years old, the turtle can mate. The female comes ashore to dig a nest for her eggs.

This diagram shows the life cycle of a turtle, from egg to adult.

In the Sandpit

Loggerhead turtles dig their nests just above the **high tide line,** where the ocean does not reach. This means the eggs will stay dry. The nest holding the eggs begins about 1 foot (30 centimeters) below the surface of the sand. Inside there are usually about 120 leathery white eggs. Each one is the size of a ping-pong ball.

The female turtle digs her nest on a sandy beach.

Inside the egg

Inside each egg is the beginnings of a turtle, called an **embryo.** For eight to nine weeks, the embryo soaks up the egg's food store, or yolk. It grows from a tiny speck into a baby turtle. The leathery wall of the egg lets in air, so that the embryo can begin to breathe. Like other **reptiles** that live in the sea, the turtle will need to breathe air for the rest of its life.

The turtle eggs look like leathery ping-pong balls.

Cool boys, warm girls

The **temperature** of the nest is very important. It affects whether the baby turtles will be boys or girls. Low temperatures make male turtles, and high temperatures make females. The turtles lay their eggs in warm **climates** so that there will be plenty of females to lay new eggs in the future.

Hatching Out

A couple of months after being laid, the eggs **hatch.** Like all baby **reptiles,** loggerheads have a special tooth called the egg tooth. This is sharp enough to cut through the egg's leathery shell. It falls off soon after the turtle hatches.

Almost there! The hatchling's head and flippers appear first.

Daring diggers

Now the **hatchlings** face a bigger challenge, because they are buried alive. Luckily all the babies in the nest hatch at the same time. They work together, using their flippers as shovels. Each hatchling is only about 2 inches (5 centimeters) long. It can take them a few days to dig through all of the sand above them. They will wait for the safety of darkness before breaking through the surface.

Nest-mates reach the surface around the same time.

Nesting season

Most nesting takes place during the summer, when the sun will keep the sand warm. This means that the eggs are ready to hatch in late summer.

Race to Safety

Loggerhead parents do not wait near the nest to help their young. **Hatchlings** must find their own way to the shore. They head for the brightest part of the sky. This is a good guide to finding the ocean, even at night.

There's no time to lose. **Predators,** or hunters, gather around turtle beaches. The biggest dangers on the beach are crabs and seagulls. In the shallow water near the shore, there are small, hungry sharks.

The hatchlings race down the beach toward the ocean.

Heading toward light

The ocean looks bright in the moonlight, but if there are lights from buildings near the beach the hatchlings can be confused. They may head the wrong way and be caught by predators. On some turtle beaches, it is against the law to have lights on at night during nesting season.

Wave goodbye

Using their flippers the hatchlings flap and crawl down the beach as fast as they can. As the first wave picks them up, the hatchlings swim for the safety of the open water. Their tiny shells are the perfect shape for slipping through water.

The hatchlings try to catch a wave that will carry them out to the ocean.

Home on the Waves

The baby turtle is at home in the ocean right away. It can hold its breath only for a short time, so it does not dive far below the surface. It has a good sense of smell, however. It uses this and other tricks to help find its way around. It can even "read" wave patterns to figure out how far from land it is and where food might be.

The color of a turtle's back helps it to hide from overhead predators such as seagulls.

Crafty camouflage

The turtle's coloring helps it to blend in with seaweed when seen from above. Seen from below, the lighter coloring on its belly makes it hard to spot against the bright surface of the sea. This **camouflage** hides the turtle from **predators.** Long flippers help it to cruise through the water. They also help the turtle speed up quickly if it is in danger.

The turtle's pale underside helps to keep it safe from predators coming from below.

Drinking water

Like every living creature, the young turtle needs to drink. There is so much salt in ocean water that drinking it would make many animals sick. However, the turtle has a special **gland** that gets rid of the salt.

The Lost Years

There are more **predators** around the coastline, so the young loggerhead turtle stays out in the open ocean while it is growing. This time is sometimes called "the lost years," because turtle experts often lose track of the young turtles.

The turtle probably spends its lost years among huge floating rafts of seaweed out in the open ocean.

Off track

The turtle travels thousands of miles during this time. It drifts along with huge clumps of seaweed, which collect around the edges of big ocean **currents.** Atlantic turtles might drift along the Gulf Stream from the Bahamas all the way over to the Mediterranean Sea. Little is known about what happens to Pacific turtles at this stage.

The young, growing turtle feeds on plenty of seaweed.

Family differences

There are two types of loggerhead turtle. One is found in the Pacific and Indian Oceans, and one is found in the Atlantic Ocean. The most visible difference between them is that the Atlantic loggerhead has two claws on each of its front flippers.

See Food, Eat Food

As the turtle grows, it can hold its breath longer and dive deeper into the ocean. It is even a better diver than many sea **mammals,** such as dolphins and killer whales. It can hold its breath for 30 minutes if it wants to chase squid or other **prey.** When it is swimming underwater the turtle closes its nostrils so that no water goes up its nose.

Turtles can eat crabs like this one, shell and all!

Pigging out

The young loggerhead is not a fussy eater. At the surface of the ocean it munches on seaweed, jellyfish, shrimp, sea snails, fish eggs, tiny plants called **algae,** and any other scraps it can find. Sadly it sometimes mistakes litter for food. Some turtles die after eating plastic bags, old balloons, or foam cups.

Tough Chew

Young loggerheads are prey to some of the ocean's biggest **predators,** like tiger sharks and killer whales. A loggerhead cannot outswim an attacking shark. But, as it grows bigger, it becomes a less attractive meal because of its thick shell.

Killer whales hunt together in groups. Their prey include sea turtles, fish, seals, penguins, and dolphins.

Hard as Nails

The young turtle's best defense is the shell around its body. This is made of two parts that grow as the turtle's body grows.

The rings on the turtle's scales tell us how old it is.

Growth rings

You can guess the age of some turtles by counting the growth rings on their scales. The turtle's scales have to grow at the same rate as its body. The age of a loggerhead is not easy to guess, however, because the rings quickly become blurry and hard to read.

Bony armor

The strongest part of the shell is the layer of bone beneath the skin. This is the same kind of bone that you have in your spine and ribs. In turtles, these have grown together to make a solid suit of armor.

On the turtle's back there is an extra layer of protection made of **scales.** This is called a carapace. Most loggerheads have ten scales in their carapace. The scales are not made of bone, but of keratin, like your fingernails.

The bony armor of this turtle's belly helps to keep it safe.

Teenage Turtles

It can take a long time for a loggerhead to grow up. Some stay in the open ocean for over ten years. Others return to coastal waters as young as six years old. They are still not old enough to become parents, but they are now about 20 inches (50 centimeters) long. This is too big to be bothered by octopuses, small sharks, and other **predators.**

As a young adult the loggerhead moves to shallow waters that are rich in food.

Life in the shallows

In warm coastal waters, there is plenty for the turtle to eat. It roams up and down the coastline, following ocean **currents** to help it on its way. It hunts along **reefs** and **lagoons,** and even explores the mouths of freshwater rivers. A reef provides shelter for the turtle to rest or hide.

Adult diet

Once it has returned to live near the shore, the turtle starts an adult diet of crabs, lobsters, sea urchins, and **shellfish** such as clams and oysters. The loggerhead's strong jaw allows it to crunch through the hard shells of its armored **prey.**

Loggerheads tear into food with their beak-like mouth.

Meeting and Mating

A turtle may be 25 to 30 years old before it is ready to **mate.** Then it leaves its feeding grounds and makes the long journey back to the beach where it was born. This is called **migration.** The turtle's long journey can be over 6,200 miles (10,000 kilometers), and may take one year or more.

Turtle get-together

The loggerheads gather at the nesting grounds in early summer and stay for about two weeks. This is the only time that loggerheads get together. They spend the rest of their lives alone.

The turtle's journey to its nesting grounds can take longer than a year.

Mating

The male attracts the female by touch. He grips her so that she cannot swim away, sometimes leaving claw marks on her shell. He curls his tail around the back of her shell and releases his **sperm.** The female stores the sperm to **fertilize** her eggs with later.

Female turtles often have scratch marks on their shells. These are made by males during mating.

Food shortage

Loggerhead turtles do not feed while they are migrating and mating. They live off stored fat in their bodies. They do not eat again until they return to their feeding grounds.

Back to the Beach

After **mating,** male loggerheads return to their feeding grounds. The females are left behind, each having some male **sperm.** Each female uses some to **fertilize** her first batch of eggs.

One night the female swims to the beach and crawls out onto the sand. It is hard work for an animal that is as heavy as two grown people, but she manages to pull herself along with her flippers. She leaves a wide track behind her.

The female starts to make her way up the beach.

High and dry

If all is well, she will climb past the **high tide line** to where the sand is dry and warm. There she will make her first nest. If the beach seems too busy or noisy, she may turn back to the sea and try again the next night.

The heavy female turtles leave tracks behind them in the sand.

Nifty Nesting

Once she has found a good nesting site, the female loggerhead uses her flippers to sweep a big circle in the sand. With her back limbs, she scoops out a hole. She drops a **clutch** of 50 to 150 eggs into the hole.

Batches of eggs

The female buries the eggs and smoothes the sand to hide her nest. She will come back to shore in two weeks' time to lay another clutch. After laying eggs three or four times, she has used up all the stored **sperm.** She will then return to her feeding grounds.

The female drops the eggs into the nest one by one.

It may be four years before she is strong enough to cope with another nesting season. But turtles can live as long as 100 years, so she has plenty of time. The turtle eggs **hatch** a couple of months after they are laid, and the **life cycle** begins all over again.

On this nesting beach, netting protects the turtles' nests from humans and animal predators.

Eggs in danger

Before the life cycle can begin again, the eggs must survive egg thieves, such as raccoons, opossums, and foxes. Although each nest is well hidden, many are raided.

Find Out for Yourself

Unless you are lucky enough to live near a turtle beach, it is probably best to find out more about loggerhead turtles by looking on the Internet and reading more books.

Books to read

Laskey, Elizabeth. *Sea Creatures: Sea Turtles*. Chicago: Heinemann, 2003.

Scarce, Carolyn. *Lifecycles Migration: The Journey of a Turtle*. London: Franklin Watts, 2000.

Using the Internet

Explore the Internet to find out more about turtles. Websites can change, so if some of the links below no longer work, don't worry. Use a search engine such as www.yahooligans.com, and type in keywords such as "loggerhead," "hatchling," and "life cycle."

Websites

www.turtles.org/kids.htm

A great site with stories and photos of real turtles, plus a webcam.

www.cccturtle.org

A wildlife protection website with useful information and pictures of turtles from all over the world.

Glossary

algae simple, one-celled plants

camouflage coloring or marks on an animal that match its surroundings, making it hard for predators to find them

climate average weather and temperature of a place

clutch group of eggs

current flow of water moving in one direction

embryo baby animal before it has been born or hatched from an egg

fertilize join together male and female parts to create a new living thing

gland organ that works like a strainer

hatch when a young animal comes out of its egg

hatchling young turtle that has just come out of its egg

high tide line highest point on a beach that the tide usually reaches

lagoon small "ocean lake," cut off from the rest of the ocean by coral reefs or sand bars

life cycle all the different stages in the life of a living thing, such as an animal or plant

mammal animal that has fur or hair, and that gives birth to its young and feeds them on milk. Seals and humans are mammals.

mate when a male and female animal come together to make eggs or babies

migration regular journey from one habitat to another

reef underwater structure, built up from sand, rocks, or the skeletons of millions of tiny creatures called coral

reptile cold-blooded animal that has a bony skeleton and scaly skin. Turtles, snakes, lizards, and crocodiles are all types of reptile.

predator animal that hunts other animals and eats them for food

prey animal that is hunted by other animals for food

scale one of the tough plates on a turtle's shell

shellfish sea creatures that have a hard shell that protects their soft, boneless bodies

skeleton bones that make up an animal's body

sperm male sex cells

temperature how hot or cold something is

Index